OH, BROTHER!

Belly Laughs for Good-Humored Catholics

BROTHER LOUGHLAN SOFIELD, ST

acta
PUBLICATIONS

OH, BROTHER!
Belly Laughs for Good-Humored Catholics
by Brother Loughlan Sofield, ST
with a Foreword by Helen Osman

Edited by Patricia A. Lynch and Gregory F. Augustine Pierce
Design and typesetting by Patricia A. Lynch
Cover art © lavatrei, Bigstock

Published by ACTA Publications, 4848 N. Clark Street, Chicago, IL 60640, (800) 397-2282, www.actapublications.com

Library of Congress Catalog number: 2014958956
ISBN: 978-0-87946-535-3
Printed in the United States of America by Total Printing Systems
Year 25 24 23 22 21 20 19 18 17 16 15
Printing 15 14 13 12 11 10 9 8 7 6 5 4 3 2 First

♻ Text printed on 30% post-consumer recycled paper

CONTENTS

DEDICATION

To Sister Carroll Juliano, SHCJ,
who has, with extraordinary patience,
listened to my stories
over and over and over...
and over.

FOREWORD HO!

———•———

Laughter has been called the best medicine and a balm for the soul, as important as love, the universal language, and something only humans can do.

Funny, isn't it, that a book of jokes can be important for our well-being? Scientists and counselors tell us that it's good for body and mind to experience a belly laugh or a wry comment on a regular basis.

Others wise in spiritual matters state that God gave us a sense of humor because it's good for our souls as well.

Dorothy Day speaks eloquently of the discipline of gratitude, but I'm sure Dorothy loved a good laugh as much as any of us. I find it hard to be grateful without laughing. The sheer fact that God created us—with our foibles as well as our gifts—should make us grin from ear to ear with delight and gratitude.

I pray this book will give you the same "heavenly" reward it has already given me.

Helen Osman
Secretary of Communications
United States Conference of Catholic Bishops

INTRODUCTION

Many years ago I attended my first Broadway play entitled *The Subject Was Roses* by Frank Gilroy. I remember sitting in the upper balcony, mesmerized by Gilroy's mastery of language. As I listened to the dialog, I was completely absorbed and could feel the tension building within me. I began to notice that when the tension built to a point where it was beginning to be overpowering, one of the actors would deliver a humorous line. The laughter released the pressure, and I was again able to focus on the play. I believe that was the day I learned the power of humor and laughter.

I have had the privilege of ministering in almost three hundred dioceses on six continents. What I learned that day on Broadway has had a strong impact on my presentations. Often the material I am covering is extremely intense. I have learned that a little humor or a joke can defuse the intensity and allow participants to absorb more of the heavy material.

St. John Paul II once commented that when you look through the scriptures, there are two elements characteristic of Jesus: healing and forgiveness. It is my conviction that I am able to be a disciple of healing when I can bring laughter, joy, and humor into the lives of those who experience great pain and suffering. Laughter is the medicine which provides spiritual and emotional healing to those who suffer. Humor and laughter are powerful tools that break down barriers and serve as the universal humanizer of us all.

In his first apostolic exhortation, *The Joy of the Gospel*, Pope Francis emphasizes the need for joy in the Christian life. He dismisses those who are joyless and lacking in humor when he says,

"Consequently, an evangelizer must never look like someone who has just come back from a funeral." He also reminds us that we are called to share our joy because the Church grows "by attraction." Throughout his exhortation, Pope Francis evokes great imagery, for example: "There are Christians whose lives seem like Lent without Easter." The true evangelizer, he reminds us, reflects joy, laughter, and happiness.

Robert Ellsberg, in *The Saints' Guide to Happiness* (New York: North Point Press, 2003, xi), says that the saints "in general...were renowned for their balance and good humor...and their ability to find joy in all things."

Once when working in the Holy Land (I presume you all realize that the Holy Land is Ireland), I was at a prayer service where the leader showed a video that revealed Jesus laughing loudly and raucously as he playfully rolled on the ground with children. I remember my immediate reaction: "Why don't we see more of that?" Too often Jesus is presented as a super stoic, seemingly devoid of joy and yet in the Gospel of John, we are reminded of the very reason for which he has come, "I have come that you may have life and have it to the fullest" (John 10:10). Life and joy and laughter are related. They may even be synonymous.

A large number of the jokes included in this book are actually true stories—funny, delightful, and sometimes poignant incidents that have happened to me and to friends. The remaining jokes are ones that I have heard during my lifetime. Their authorship is unknown, and I simply thank anyone who sees one of his or her jokes in this book. It is impossible to track down their initial authorship.

One final thought. You don't stop laughing because you grow old. You grow old because you stop laughing.

Brother Loughlan Sofield, ST

OH, BROTHER!

For several evenings at bedtime, Mrs. Smith had been teaching the Lord's Prayer to her three-year-old daughter, Veronica. Mrs. Smith would recite the prayer, one line at a time, and Veronica would faithfully repeat the words.

Finally, Veronica decided to go solo. She carefully enunciated each word, until she got to the last phrase. "Lead us not into temptation," she concluded, "but deliver us from email."

"Amen," said her mom.

A mother had three sons, two of the boys belonging to the same religious community.

She was fond of confusing people by saying, "I have three sons, and two of them are brothers."

Brother Loughlan was conducting a program for diocesan pastoral leaders. Trying to cover a massive amount of material in a rather short period of time, he was visibly frustrated. "I feel like a mosquito in a nudist colony," he declared. "Where do I begin?"

The parish custodian was wiped out at the end of one horrendous winter day. Hoping to reduce some of his stress, he emailed the weather anchor at one of the local TV stations. "Just for the record," he wrote, "I have just finished shoveling six inches of your 'partly cloudy.'"

She emailed him back, "Wait until you see my 'light flurries' tonight."

Lyle and Lucy, an elderly couple from Our Lady of Perpetual Help Parish, spent their later years in a senior living facility. One day Lucy sent her husband to the dining hall to get her some ice cream. Knowing he was getting more and more forgetful, she demanded he make a list. "I want a strawberry sundae with two scoops of ice cream," she said.

Just as Lyle was getting ready to leave, Lucy called him back and added, "And I want chocolate syrup and lots of whipped cream. Now write that all down."

Obediently, Lyle wrote it all down.

When Lyle returned an hour later, he handed Lucy a tray with scrambled eggs, bacon, sausage, and coffee.

"What is this?" she scolded. "Where's the toast?"

An elderly woman walked into St. Veronica's for the 10 a.m. Mass. The young usher greeted her at the door and asked her where she'd like to sit.

When she told him she'd like to sit in the front row, he walked her down the aisle. When they got there he whispered, "I wouldn't recommend this."

"Why not?" she asked.

"The pastor is really boring," he replied.

"Do you know who I am?" the woman asked.

"No," he said.

"I'm the pastor's mother."

"Do you know who I am?" he asked.

"No," she said. "Should I?"

"Not at all," he said before making a beeline for the back of church.

The pastoral associate told one of her parishioners that she had been praying for patience and understanding with her pastor but recently had discontinued her prayer. She was afraid God might grant it.

Notre Dame High School for Boys was having its annual picnic.

Three students were walking near the lake when they heard someone shouting for help. Not far away they saw the local mayor, an unpopular leader who was against parochial schools, splashing around in the middle of the lake. He was close to drowning. All three boys jumped in the water to save him.

When they were successfully back on land, the mayor thanked them profusely and asked if there was anything that he could do for them.

The first said he would like an appointment to the Naval Academy in Annapolis. The mayor promised him that he would try to arrange that.

The second asked for an appointment to West Point. The mayor said he would try to grant that wish as well.

The mayor turned to the third young man and asked if he had a request. "Yes," he said, "I would like to be buried at Arlington National Cemetery."

Surprised, the mayor asked why a man so young would be making such a strange request.

"Because," the student responded, "when the principal finds out I saved your life, he's going to kill me."

After Sunday Mass, a parishioner stopped to talk with Deacon Steve. "Your homily reminded me of the Washington monument," he said. "It took a long time to get to the point!"

An elderly brother with a reputation for being less than zealous reported to his hardworking superior.

"I'd like to retire," the brother said.

Incredulous, the superior inquired, "From what?"

"I've got some good news," Mother Superior announced to her community. "Sister Rita is recovering so well from her heart surgery that the doctor says she can begin working one day a week."

One of the sisters turned to the sister closest to her and said, "That means they just cut Mother Superior's work load in half."

At the beginning of Mass, Father Juan, realizing someone might notice, announced that he had cut his neck. While shaving that morning, he explained, he had been concentrating on his homily.

After Mass one of his parishioners shook the priest's hand, saying with all seriousness, "Next time, Father, think about your neck and cut your talk."

During a rather long and boring homily at a children's Mass, Sister Janet, the principal, observed Little Jonnie, a small, first-grade boy, standing up in his front-row pew and talking with the children in the row behind him. Sister waved at him, trying to communicate to him that his behavior was inappropriate, but Little Jonnie simply smiled at her and waved back.

Annoyed, the principal turned to Little Janie sitting next to her and instructed her, "Go and tell him to stop talking and sit down."

Obediently, the girl walked up the side aisle, past the front row, and into the sanctuary, where she whispered in the priest's ear, "Sister said to stop talking and sit down."

The priest, a graduate of Catholic grade school, immediately sat down and shut up.

At a parish woman's retreat, participants shared their own gifts and then identified the gifts of the other members of their small group.

One woman was the last one to share in her small group of women. The others in the group were effusive, recounting all the gifts they saw in her.

Finally, the woman responded, "Say, would one of you mind giving my husband a quick call and let him know I'm too good for him?"

Liz, the religious education director, hung a banner in her office that read, "The truth will set you free. But first it will make you miserable."

An octogenarian couple in the parish approached their equally elderly pastor emeritus and informed him that they wanted to get married—both for the first time.

"Why now?" the priest asked them, more quizzically than seriously.

"We want to have an heir," the couple told him in unison.

The priest was perplexed. How was he going to inform the couple that they were no longer heir-conditioned?

———

During the installation of the new bishop, the papal nuncio spoke glowingly of him, but he added a sad note. "Unfortunately," he said, "our new bishop's mother died recently and is not here for the occasion."

The new bishop, his eyes now filled with tears, was then expected to make some remarks. Standing in front of the assembly in his full regalia, including his mitre, all he could manage to say was, "Maybe it's for the best. Mom always told me never to wear my hat in church."

———

Before Mass began, the pastor informed the congregation that he and the bishop had been in an intense process of discernment to determine the priest's future. "As a result," the priest announced to everyone, "it seems to be the will of Jesus that I be assigned to another parish."

The priest assured the congregation that he would share more about the decision in his homily and then signaled the organist to begin the opening hymn. He was a little surprised to hear "What a Friend We Have in Jesus."

Father Bob, a fire-and-brimstone preacher, proclaimed, "If you do not repent, you will go to hell where there will be weeping and gnashing of teeth."

Directly in front of him was an elderly, well-dressed lady. Throughout his tirade she just sat there, grinning broadly.

The priest, thinking she must not have heard him, looked directly at her and repeated, "There will be weeping and gnashing of teeth."

Much to his dismay, the woman just kept on grinning.

Father Bob became so frustrated that he stepped away from the pulpit, walked down the sanctuary steps, and stood directly in front of her.

With even greater vehemence he shouted, "There will be weeping and gnashing of teeth!"

"But Father," she said as she looked him right in the eye, "I don't have any teeth!"

With that he became so flustered that he shouted out to the rest of the congregation, "Teeth will be provided!"

The next Sunday, Father Bob proclaimed in his booming voice, "One day everyone from this parish will die."

Finding himself face-to-face with the same grinning, toothless, elderly lady, he wondered how she could possibly resist this stern warning.

"Father," she cheerfully responded from her front-row pew, "I'm not from this parish."

———•———

After God created man, he said, "I can do better than this."

A woman sitting next to Brother Louis on a plane kept looking over his shoulder and finally asked if he were a Catholic. When he responded in the affirmative, she asked if the Church still taught the same things she had learned as a child. Not quite sure where this was leading, Brother Louis asked her what she had in mind.

"I was wondering," the woman said. "Do we still have mortal sin and congenial sin?"

"Some mortal sins," Brother Louis informed her, "are more congenial than others."

———

Before his homily, the deacon announced to the congregation, "My job is to speak, and yours is to listen. If you finish your job before I finish mine, please raise your hand."

Every hand in the church immediately went up.

———

Little Jonnie had his own version of one of the lines of the Lord's Prayer. "And forgive us our trash baskets," he prayed, "as we forgive those who put trash in our baskets."

———

At a conference, a psychiatrist was discussing his book on Irish Catholic guilt.

A member of the audience asked if Irish guilt was different from other Catholic experiences of guilt.

"No," the psychiatrist responded, "apparently it is just less motivational."

At Sunday Mass, one of the ushers noticed that a man sitting in the front pew had not removed his hat.

He approached the man and asked him to remove it, but the man ignored the usher and continued to pray his rosary.

The usher returned with the head usher who explained to the man that church etiquette demanded that he not wear his hat in church. The head usher was ignored as well.

So the head usher summoned the priest, who confronted the man in the same way.

At last the man responded and explained. "I've been coming to this church for years, Father, and the only time anyone ever talks to me is when I keep my hat on."

———•———

A superior of a men's religious order was asked if many of his men were suffering from burnout.

"No," he responded, without giving it a second thought. "Our problem is ignition."

———•———

A rather rotund bishop traveled to Rome for his *ad limina* visit with the pope.

During lunch, the pope asked how things were going in the bishop's diocese.

When the bishop indicated that his flock was growing, the pope whispered innocently to the cardinal next to him, "The food is apparently very good there."

The members of St. John the Baptist Parish had put in months of preparation for their twenty-fifth anniversary. Every committee had worked overtime, but only one committee—the liturgy committee—had experienced a high level of anxiety. It was this committee's responsibility to invite the celebrant—the local bishop. Everyone knew the bishop had a short fuse, exploding at even minor provocations.

During the jubilee liturgy, the pastor, who was sitting to the right of the bishop, observed that the bishop was glaring at the congregation during the proclamation of the gospel, which happened to be about the beheading of John the Baptist.

When it came time for the offertory procession, a beautiful and graceful professional dancer led the gift-bearers down the center aisle.

The pastor observed the bishop glaring at her as well. In his anxiety, he quietly whispered, "Well, bishop, what do you think?"

"If she asks me for your head on a platter," he replied, "she has it."

The newly-elected provincial of an order of women religious called her elderly mother to share the news of her new position of responsibility in the community.

"That's nice, honey," her mother replied. "Didn't anyone else want it?"

The instructor at the parish workshop on aging shared the following pearls of wisdom:

- Remember the five *Bs* of aging men: bifocals, bridges, bunions, balding, and bulging.
- Just because you have silver in your hair and gold in your teeth, doesn't mean you have green in your wallet.
- Aging women never get lonely because they have so many men in their lives: Will Power, Charlie Horse, Arthur Ritis, Ben Gay, and—of course—Stretch Pants.
- You know you are getting old when the majority of names in your personal phone book end in *MD*.

———·———

Father Jose was an avid soccer fan and had season tickets for the local soccer team. The team, however, was having a horrible season, the worst in decades.

One Sunday, the priest added this personal announcement at the end of Mass.

"I was going to tell you I had two tickets for the next soccer game on the dashboard of my car in case someone wanted to come with me," he said, "but in the meantime someone broke in and now there are four."

———·———

St. John XXIII once explained that there are several ways to lose money: carousing, gambling, and farming.

"My father," he said, "chose the most boring of the three."

An elderly bishop preferred to put everything in writing instead of dealing with people directly.

Whenever the bishop went on vacation, his staff referred to it as his memo-pause.

———•———

An elderly parishioner approached the young associate after Mass, sharing, "You don't know how much your homilies mean to my husband since he's lost his mind."

———•———

Those who wish to become effective preachers should heed advice based on a legend of the great Greek statesman Demosthenes: Fill up your mouth with marbles. Then take all the marbles out, one at a time. When you've lost all your marbles, you are ready to preach.

———•———

When it was announced that his flight was delayed, an irate monsignor bypassed the long line at the ticket counter, screamed at the agent, and demanded to be put on the next plane to his destination.

In a soft voice, the agent asked him to go to the end of the line, explaining that she would deal with him in turn.

In response, the monsignor banged his fists on the counter and in a loud, belligerent voice asked, "Do you know who I am?"

Patiently, the agent picked up the microphone. "We have a priest here who doesn't know who he is," she announced. "Is there anyone who can help him?"

Sheila, the director of adult formation, shared a story about Oliver Wendell Holmes, the great but absent-minded American jurist, in her presentation on the Catholic Church and the United States government.

It seems that one day Justice Holmes boarded a train.

A few minutes later the conductor approached his compartment, shouting, "Tickets! Tickets!" When he received no response from Mr. Holmes, he opened that door and again shouted, "Ticket!"

Justice Holmes was frantically searching his brief case and jacket pockets, but could not find his ticket.

Seeing the judge's consternation and knowing his reputation, the conductor reassured him. "Don't worry, Your Honor" he said. "When you arrive at your destination, just put the ticket in an envelope and send it to the company."

Justice Holmes stood up to his full stature. "My good man," he declared, "you do not seem to understand the severity of the problem. The problem is not whether or not I have a ticket. The question is, where am I going?"

———

The bishop of New Orleans regularly said Mass for a small community of cloistered nuns.

Every time he arrived, the portress would greet him and the bishop would ask her to pray for the Saints, his favorite football team.

And every time, she made the same reply with the sweetest smile. "I do, Bishop," she would say, "but I'm not sure they need it anymore."

Brother Cyril, a visiting lecturer, was introduced to the class by Susan, the adult formation minister, as "a very warm person."

"Initially," said Brother Cyril, "I thought that was a beautiful introduction. But since I have my dictionary handy, I looked it up only to discover that *warm* is defined as 'not so hot.'"

Totally embarrassed, Susan assured him and the members of the class that she meant the introduction in a very positive way. "The reason that we invited you to speak," she explained, "is because you are a role model on the topic we are addressing."

Out of curiosity, Brother Cyril opened his dictionary again. "I see," he said. "According to the dictionary, a *model* is 'small imitation of the real thing.'"

Susan responded, "While you're at it, Brother, why don't you look up *insufferable*?"

———

Depending on which group of parishioners you consult, you'll end up with a different impression of the pastor.

- One group perceives him as a man who has become a legend in his own time.
- The other group identifies him as a man who has become a legend in his own mind.

———

The Ladies Sodality sponsored a wine and cheese social featuring a special Scottish cheese—Loch Ness Muenster.

A parishioner approached Father Dan and informed him she was contemplating a divorce.

"Do you have sufficient grounds for a divorce?" he asked.

"Yes," the woman responded, "we have four acres."

Father Dan was confused. "Do you or your husband hold a grudge in your marriage?"

"Of course!" the woman replied. "We have a two-car grudge. He puts his car in one, and I put mine in the other."

The frustrated cleric then asked, "Well, does he beat you up?"

"No," she replied, "I get up before him every morning."

In utter desperation, Father Dan tried once more. "Do you happen to wake up grumpy in the morning?"

"No," she answered, "I let him sleep."

Finally he had to ask the obvious. "Are you sure you want a divorce?"

"It's not me," she snapped. "It's my husband. He thinks we have a communication problem."

A bishop began the continuing education program for clergy by declaring that he had a very important announcement. "As of today," he said, "celibacy will be optional."

Now that he had his priests' complete attention, he added, "...for anyone sitting in the front row."

Church bulletin announcement: "Please pray for John Jay, who passed away on March 2 at the request of his sister."

Father Paul was overheard asking a parishioner if he thought the pastor had the right to make the final decisions for the parish.

When the parishioner answered in the affirmative, Father Paul informed him, "Well, I'm glad to inform you that you are now on the pastoral council."

The sign in front of St. Mary's Church read:

• Morning service—Jesus walks on the water.
• Evening service—the search for Jesus.

Little Jonnie came home from school one day and proudly announced to his parents, "Today we learned how to make babies."

His parents were shocked. Reluctantly, they asked their son to explain what he had learned.

"You drop the *y*," Billy responded, "and add *ies*."

A long-winded Bible scholar was conversing with one of his confreres.

Finally the friend interrupted him. "Skip creation, Karl," he suggested, "and start with the rapture."

The only people who find what they are looking for in life are the fault-finders.

Father Justin was struggling to help his parish council grasp the need for a new rectory. Finally, he thought of a way to make his point.

Citing the shortage of priests in the diocese, he informed them that within a few years there might not be any priest regularly assigned to the parish, especially if the parish did not have a suitable rectory.

"A priest might have to be flown in by helicopter each Sunday," he continued. "Is that what you want?"

The council spent the rest of the meeting discussing where to build the helicopter pad.

———·———

"The pastor has no patience," said his secretary. "I mean it! He has a serious wait problem."

———·———

Father Domingo was celebrating Mass for the second graders. He pointed to the large *chi rho* (XP) on his vestments and asked if any of the children knew what it meant.

Most of the children were dumbfounded, but Little Jonnie kept waving his hand and shouting, "I know! I know!"

Finally, Father Domingo called on him. "What does the *chi rho* mean, Little Jonnie?"

Little Jonnie announced with pride, "No parking!"

———·———

No good deed goes unpunished.
It's the bad ones we're not sure about.

A certain bishop had a reputation for his inability to remember names.

His staff, trying to save him from embarrassment, devised a way to help. Whenever he was scheduled to visit a parish or attend a meeting, they supplied him with a single index card with the names of the significant people he might encounter at a particular event.

At a meeting at Our Lady of the Lake Parish, the bishop praised the pastor profusely, glancing at his index card and correctly naming the pastor.

He then did the exact same thing for the principal, checking his card before identifying her by name.

Feeling pretty satisfied with himself, he ended his presentation by declaring, "But remember, we owe it all to our Lord and Savior uh, uh, uh..."

Flustered, the bishop consulted his card, breathed a sigh of relief, and said, "Jesus Christ!"

———

Father Frank began the liturgy by announcing, "There's something wrong with this microphone."

One of the older members of the congregation replied semi-automatically, "And with your spirit."

———

From a church bulletin: "The healing Mass scheduled for this week has been cancelled because the celebrant has malaria."

Liz, the director of religious education, was heard to exclaim, "Necessity is the mother of theology."

———————

Brother Howard, a novice in his community, attended a conference on poverty. When he registered at the front desk, he was told his room had a king-size bed, a hot tub, and a beautiful view of the city. He also discovered he had full access to room service. When the food was delivered, it was still very hot and delicious.

During the many breaks at the conference, participants were served fine wine, fresh fruit, and a variety of flavorful cheeses.

"If this is poverty," Brother Howard wrote on his evaluation form, "bring on celibacy."

———————

There once were two boll weevils.
One went to New York and got rich.
The other stayed home toiling in the fields.
He was, of course, the lesser of the two weevils.

———————

Flying home to his diocese, the bishop was attempting to get his bag into the overhead rack.

One of the other passengers helped him and then joked, "Will this get me to heaven, Your Excellency?"

"Not on this flight, I hope," the bishop responded.

Jesus asked his disciples, "Who do you say that I am?"

Peter responded simply, "You are the Messiah, the Son of the Living God."

There are some who believe that if Jesus were to pose that same question to some theologians today, they might respond, "You are the eschatological manifestation of the kerygma of our very being, the ultimate signification in which we see meaning in our interpersonal relations."

To which Peter (and probably Jesus) would respond, "Huh?"

———•———

At a rural parish school in Australia, the religion teacher was just a bit taken aback when one of her students reported that Jesus had been crucified by a Qantas pilot.

———•———

After finishing up a parish mission, the priest was being driven to his next assignment by an older deacon who very proudly described himself as having the gift of listening.

"That's great," said the priest. "What did you think of what I said this week?"

"I'm not sure," said the deacon. "I'm hard of hearing and really couldn't catch much of what you said."

———•———

Sister Patricia, a popular motivational speaker, was invited to preach a mission on "the parish as a welcoming community."

When she arrived at the airport, no one was there to meet her.

Three Catholics were to be guillotined: a romantic Frenchman, a cynical Russian, and a know-it-all American.

The Frenchman was the first to approach the guillotine. When asked if he had any final words, he declared, "I have led a good life. I have feasted on the finest French food and wines. I have enjoyed the beauty of the French countryside. I am ready to die." Without waiting to be ordered to do so, he placed his head down on the block, and the guillotine dropped. A foot above his head, the blade stopped, and the crowd shouted, "It's a miracle!" His captors were forced to release him.

The Russian, asked for his final words, declared, "I have been cold, and I have been hungry. It doesn't matter to me whether I live or die." He also placed his head on the block. Again, the blade dropped, stopping just a foot above his head. And again, the people cried, "It's a miracle!" The Russian also was released.

Finally, it came time for the American. When he was asked for his final words, he declared, "I watched the first two times, and I think if you loosen the top two screws the thing will work perfectly."

Raymond and Barbara, a senior married couple, were sipping wine at the parish picnic.

Suddenly, Barbara whispered softly and tenderly, "I love you so much. I don't know how I could ever live without you."

Raymond looked over at his wife. "Is that you or the wine talking?" he asked.

"It's me," responded Barbara, "talking to the wine."

A missionary brother had been stranded on an island for eighteen months.

Suddenly, a voluptuous woman wearing a wet-suit arrived. Cuddling up to him, she asked, "When was the last time you played around?"

The missionary became animated and responded, "You brought some golf clubs?"

———·———

An elderly woman from the parish discovered that one of the radio stations was offering a free hearing test. All listeners had to do to take the test was to call a special number.

A few days later, the parish nurse asked her if she had taken the test and how she had done.

"I called," she said, "but they couldn't understand one thing I was saying. So I just hung up."

"Oh, you must have called the chancery by mistake," said the nurse.

———·———

A rabbi and a priest and a nun were enjoying lunch at an interfaith meeting.

"This ham is delicious," the priest joked. "I can't understand how anything so wonderful could be forbidden by religious law. Come on, Rabbi, when are you going to try it?"

Without missing a beat, the Rabbi responded. "I'll try it," she said with a wide grin, "at your wedding or sister's ordination."

Four priests, who were in the same class at the seminary, got together every year on the anniversary of their ordination.

On their twenty-fifth anniversary, they met at a fancy restaurant. Midway through the meal, they noticed that one of their number had become silent and withdrawn. When they asked him what was happening, he tearfully told them that he believed he might have a drinking problem.

The others immediately offered their support, assuring him they would see that he received whatever treatment he needed and would be present and supportive.

After a short pause, one of the other priests commented on the fact that in all their years of meeting they had never before talked about such matters. He then admitted he might have a gambling problem. He had been taking money from the collection to bet at the track.

Again, the others were completely supportive.

Yet another, overwhelmed by their honesty and support, shared he might be falling in love with the parish secretary.

Again, complete support from the group.

Finally, they turned to face the fourth classmate and asked whether he was dealing with any problems.

He assured them that he wasn't. "Except," he disclosed, "I'm the biggest gossip in town."

A couple of elderly parishioners observed Deacon Bill preparing his homily in a corner of the parish hall.

"Isn't that nice," one of them said. "He practices what he preaches."

Fathers Greg and Ernesto were driving through Maine on their vacation. They had been classmates in the seminary and had always been competitive.

When they saw a sign directing them toward the town of Calais, they became embroiled in an argument about the correct pronunciation of the town's name. The argument became increasingly intense. Neither would give in.

When they arrived in Calais, they pulled into a shopping center. Entering one of the shops, Father Greg gruffly demanded of the young woman at the counter, "Tell us how to pronounce the name of this place. Go slow and be very clear."

Somewhat nervously but very carefully the girl complied: "Dun...kin'...Do...nuts."

———

A priest, a minister, and a guru were engaged in a discussion about the best position for prayer.

A telephone repairman in the adjacent room listened as he worked on the phone line.

"Kneeling," declared the priest, "is the best way to pray."

The minister stated, "The best way to pray is standing with hands lifted toward heaven."

The guru chimed in next. "You're both wrong," he said. "I pray in a prone position with my eyes closed."

At this point, the repairman interrupted their conversation and added his two cents. "The best way I ever prayed," he said, "was when I was hanging upside down from a telephone pole."

Agatha Christie, the mystery writer, was married to a biblical archeologist who spent much of his time excavating relics. When asked what it was like to be married to a man like that, she answered, "It's wonderful. The older I get, the more interesting he finds me."

———·———

A missionary had such complete trust in God that every day as he went on his pastoral rounds he took nothing for protection. No gun, no knife.

One day, as he stepped out into a clearing in the jungle, he saw a huge lion, crouched and ready to pounce. Immediately, the missionary fell on his knees, folded his hands, and lifted his head toward heaven in fervent prayer, asking God to protect him.

After a couple of seconds, when the lion still had not devoured him, the missionary lifted his head. To his amazement the lion was kneeling in front of him, paws folded and head lifted heavenward, apparently in prayer.

Just as the missionary was about to cry out, "Thank you, God, for sending me a Christian lion," he heard the lion praying, "Bless us, O Lord, and these thy gifts...."

———·———

An elderly parishioner was attending a wake. One of his fellow parishioners said, "It's good to see you, Tom."

"Being seen," Tom replied, "is better than being viewed."

A young couple invited their elderly pastor for dinner on Sunday evening. While they were in the kitchen preparing the meal, the pastor was left alone with their six-year-old son, Little Jonnie.

Trying to make conversation, he asked the boy, "What are we having for dinner?"

"Goat," Little Jonnie replied.

Surprised, the pastor asked, "Are you sure about that?"

"Yes," the boy replied. "I heard Dad telling Mom that today was as good as any other day to have the old goat for dinner."

When Deacon Jerry and his wife were moving to their new home it was a blistering hot day.

The movers sweated profusely during the four hours it took to pack all the belongings into the truck. Jerry commented to one of the guys on how impressed he was with their perseverance in the heat.

"It's not the heat that gets you," the man said. "It's the humility."

Jerry saved that line for his next homily on divine judgment.

The newly-ordained priest was home for his first Mass when his mother fell seriously ill.

When he asked her if there was anything he could do, she responded, "I feel terrible. Get a priest."

"Mom," he replied, "I'm a priest."

"No," she responded. "Get a *real* priest."

At the end of a busy day, the bishop was standing in the office area of the chancery next to the shredder, holding a single sheet of paper.

The diocesan director of finance saw that the bishop appeared a bit confused. "Can I help you, Excellency?" he asked.

"My secretary has already gone home," the bishop replied, "and I have no idea how to work this machine. This is a very sensitive document."

Hoping to score some brownie points, the director offered to take care of it. He placed the sheet of paper in the shredder and turned on the machine.

The bishop turned away and said, "Thanks, I only need one copy."

Deacon Tim took his wife, Maria, to a romantic restaurant to celebrate their fiftieth wedding anniversary. The furnishings were elegant, the wine and food were magnificent, and the pianist played enchanting music.

After a couple of glasses of wine, the couple joined hands visibly, moved by the music. One romantic song in particular stirred up feelings in both of them. The melody was familiar, but neither could recall the name of the song.

Finally, Tim motioned to their waitress and asked if she would find out what the pianist was playing.

"I'd be delighted," she replied and went off to ask.

"The pianist said," the waitress reported back, "that she is playing a piano."

When the bishop visited one of the multi-cultural, multilingual parishes in the diocese, Father Pedro served as his translator.

One of the parishioners, known for his long, rambling speeches, was waxing eloquently in his native tongue.

Ten minutes passed without a word of translation from Father Pedro.

The bishop turned to him and whispered, "What's he saying?"

"Don't worry," Father Pedro answered. "If he says anything important, I'll let you know."

The next week, the bishop appointed Father Pedro as the editor of the diocesan newspaper.

Willie, a young parishioner at St. Martha's Parish, was an avid hockey fan.

Every chance he could get, he would attend the home games of the local professional team. In time, he became close friends with the team's goalie.

One day the goalie invited Willie to his home for dinner. Willie was overwhelmed with the invitation. "Can I bring my father?" he asked. "He's your number one fan."

"Of course," the goalie answered.

When the evening came, they had a truly wonderful time— the father, the son, and the goalie host.

Seen on the bumper of an SUV
outside Queen of All Saints School:
"I child-proofed my house, but they still get in."

Helen, the pastoral associate, was overheard telling the rest of the staff that they had a very willing community. Some were willing to work, and the rest were willing to let them.

----·----

Father Ted was his usual grouchy self as he rushed to catch his flight to St. Louis. He made it to the plane just before the door closed, grabbed the last remaining seat, and immediately started bombarding his seat-mate with a litany of complaints.

About a half hour into the flight, the pilot announced that one of their four engines had failed and assured the passengers that there was no need to worry. "The only problem," he said, "is that we'll be about fifteen minutes late."

Fifteen minutes later, the pilot informed them that a second engine had failed. Again, he assured them that he would have no difficulty landing the plane, but they would now be about thirty minutes late.

A few minutes later, the pilot, in a high-pitched, nervous voice, notified the passengers that they had now lost a third engine. "The plane will be fine with our current equipment," he assured them. "I've been trained for just such an emergency. However, we'll now be one hour late."

The priest had been listening to these announcements and checking his watch each time. Now he was exasperated. "If we lose one more engine," he said to his neighbor, "we're probably never going to make it!"

----·----

An x-ray technician married one of her patients.
I wonder what she saw in him.

During the homily, Father Gerardo informed the congregation that he was being transferred.

After Mass he noticed a group of people crying. In an effort to console them, he said, "Don't feel bad. The bishop promised that he would send a good replacement."

The crying continued. "Yes," one parishioner finally responded, "but that's what he said the last time."

The seminarian asked his philosophy teacher the difference between ignorance and apathy.

"I don't know," the teacher said snappily, "and I don't care."

Just before Notre Dame University's annual homecoming game against Brigham Young University, some of BYU's Mormon students were seen on campus with signs that read, "Need tickets. Willing to attend Mass."

After weeks of heated discussion, the pastoral council finally hired a contractor to add a wing onto the parish hall—an atrium.

Five years and another heated discussion later, the council hired the same contractor to build another wing onto the hall—what came to be known as the b-trium.

A woman invited some friends to dinner. At the table, she turned to their six-year-old daughter and said, "Little Janie, would you like to say the blessing?"

"I don't know what to say," Little Janie protested.

"Just say what you hear Mommy say," her mother answered, encouragingly.

Obediently, Little Janie bowed her head and prayed, "Lord, why on earth did I invite all these people to dinner?"

Mary had been chosen by the pastor to sit at the bishop's table at the dinner following Confirmation. She had never personally met a bishop, and her excitement was mingled with a bit of anxiety.

When the bishop mentioned his mother, Mary responded. "Bishop," she blurted out, "it never dawned on me that a bishop would have a mother."

The bishop laughed and said, "And it probably never occurred to her that a mother might have a bishop for a son."

St. Peter's Parish finally concluded its capital campaign and moved ahead with plans for the long-awaited new church building. The pastoral council reviewed plans submitted by several architects and chose a most fitting design—a building in the shape of a fish—to honor its namesake.

Forever after, St. Peter's was known as the House of Cod.

When an affluent parish held a formal dance, a number of the women, as was their habit, tried to outdo one another.

One of the women had hired Christian Dior to design her dress and paraded around the gathering like a proud peacock.

After dinner, guests were enjoying coffee and dessert when a waiter accidently poured coffee on the proud woman's dress.

"Get out of here," she screamed at the apologetic waiter, "and never darken my Dior again."

———

Father Don, an army chaplain, returned home after spending two years in Afghanistan.

The first thing he did was change out of his uniform and into his favorite black suit.

When he reached in the coat pocket, he discovered a receipt for a pair of shoes he had dropped off at the shoemaker before he deployed. He immediately got in his car and drove to the shop.

When Father Don inquired if the shoemaker still had the shoes, the shoemaker went into the backroom to check. "Yes, I do, Father," he said. "They'll be ready next week."

———

The parish secretary was walking along the canal in Venice, California, on her lunch break. When she spotted a woman walking on the other side, she called, "How do you get to the other side?"

"You *are* on the other side," the woman called back.

Bishop Fulton Sheen liked to tell this story about himself.
He was giving a talk at a fancy New York hotel. When he returned to his room after the talk, he had the sense that someone had been in the room while he was out. Seeing that the bed had been turned down and the pillows fluffed, he realized a hotel employee had made the room welcoming for the night. The employee had even placed a gold-wrapped chocolate on each pillow.

On the bottom of one side of the bed she had laid out his pajamas.

On the bottom of the other side of the bed she had laid out his lace surplice.

———·———

Puzzling Questions
- Why does a doctor refer to his work as his practice?
- Why is a financial adviser called a broker?
- Why does an airport refer to its building as a terminal?
- Why is the one who hears the confession called the confessor?

———·———

The deacon was preaching on the evil of alcoholism. "A hangover," he declared, "is the wrath of grapes."

———·———

An announcement in the church bulletin for the last weekend in February read: "Whoever is praying for snow, please stop."

During a break in the monthly meeting of the St. Anselm's men's club, a few of the guys talked about their latest electronic gadgets.

One of the men then admitted that he was falling in love with the woman on his GPS. "She's so compassionate," he said. "She never yells at me when I make a mistake."

"Yes, that's true," said one of the other men, "and she's a lawyer."

"How do you know that?" asked the first man.

"She must be," said the second man. "She's always telling me to make a legal u-turn."

———•———

The bishop was driving home after a late-night hospital visit.

When he saw the flashing red light of a squad car in his rear-view mirror, he pulled over.

The policeman approached him, informed him that he was going fifteen miles over the speed limit, and asked for his license. After scanning his license, the policeman noticed that the bishop was required to wear glasses when driving.

The bishop replied calmly, "I have contacts, my son."

"I don't care who you know, Dad" the policeman replied sarcastically. "You're still getting a ticket."

———•———

The retired bishop celebrated a special Mass for the jubilarians of all the religious communities in his diocese. First, he asked those celebrating their seventieth and sixtieth anniversaries to come forward. Then he turned to those celebrating their golden jubilees and said, "I'll get to you kids later."

The older priest had been trying to get his live-in house-keeper to understand that household items were shared equally, but she had the habit of saying, "Father, *your* refrigerator is broken," or "Father, *your* television isn't working."

Each time she said something like this, the priest would gently and patiently remind her, "It's *our* refrigerator," or "It's *our* television."

The housekeeper resisted this way of thinking for quite some time, but she finally got it. Then, one day the bishop was paying a visit to the rectory. While the priest and the bishop were having coffee in the dining room, they were startled by a loud scream. "Father," the housekeeper shouted, "there's a mouse under *our* bed!"

The archbishop had a good sense of humor about his rotund physique.

While visiting a small rural parish, the pastor was getting ready to introduce the archbishop to a group of non-Catholics, most of whom had never seen a bishop.

"Well," the archbishop told the pastor, "they're going to see a lot of one right now."

Another time, the archbishop visited another parish for Confirmation, one of the parishioners is said to have addressed him as "Your Immensity."

**If you really want to make God laugh,
just tell him about your plans.**

Sister Felicia was feeling so ill that she asked to be taken to the emergency room. In describing her experience to the other members of the convent when she returned, she said, "I was X-rated and sent home."

———

St. Joseph's School conducted a Christmas art contest for the children in the lower grades. Little Janie, one of the first-grade children, drew a picture of the Nativity complete with Jesus, Mary, and Joseph. In the corner of the stable stood a rather obese individual.

When her teacher asked her to identify this figure, Little Janie replied, "Why, that's Round John Virgin!"

Most people don't mind if a sermon goes over their heads as long as it hits somebody else.

———

An unshaven man dressed in shabby clothes who didn't smell too good approached the pastor of a rather upscale Catholic church and asked to join the parish. The pastor, rather sheepishly, replied that presently they were not taking new members at the time and suggested that the man appeal directly to God.

Weeks later the pastor saw the man on the street. He tried to pass unseen, but the man recognized him and wanted to talk. "Father," he said, "I took your advice and talked to God and he told me not to worry about it. He said he's been trying to get into your church for over twenty years and he ain't welcome there either."

St. Elizabeth's College had finally gone co-ed, and the administration was uneasy.

At the first convocation of the year, the president followed the advice of her staff and laid out the rules. "If a man is found visiting in the women's dorm or a woman the men's dorm, both parties will be fined $25. A second violation will result in a $50 fine, and a third a $100 fine."

The president then asked if there were any questions.

One of the wise-guy sophomores raised his hand." How much is it," he asked, "for a season pass?"

———

The pastor had a call from an IRS agent inquiring if he had a parishioner by the name of John Smith.

"Yes, indeed," the priest answered. "He is a very faithful, long-time contributing member of the parish."

The IRS agent wasn't yet satisfied. "Did this John Smith," he asked, "recently give a $10,000 donation to the parish?"

The priest answered in the affirmative. "He certainly will now."

———

On their way to Mass, a catechist asked her students, "And why is it necessary to be quiet in church?"

"Because," Little Janie replied, "people are sleeping."

———

**Some people get most of their exercise
by jumping to conclusions.**

In the past, religious men and women were sternly cautioned against forming what were called "particular friendships."

One insecure young novice informed the older sisters that she would never have to worry about this. "Anyone who is particular," she said, "would never pick me as a friend."

The conference of religious vocation directors convened its quarterly meeting.

At the end of the first day, a group gathered for some liquid refreshment. Soon they became embroiled in a debate over which religious order was the best.

The Franciscans touted their community's commitment to the poor and abandoned.

The Dominicans countered with praise for their community's charism of preaching.

Others spoke glowingly of their specific apostolates.

After midnight, the party finally came to an end and each director went to his room.

When they woke in the morning, they discovered a message tacked to the bulletin board: "All orders are created equal."

It was signed "God, S.J."

Adam blamed Eve.
Eve blamed the snake.
And the snake didn't have a leg to stand on.

St. Rita's Parish was proud of attracting a large number of young families. Membership had almost doubled in five years, with a corresponding increase in the celebration of the sacraments, especially baptism and marriage.

One particular Sunday the number of babies being presented for baptism was even greater than usual. The young associate pastor seemed overwhelmed. "Because of the number of children being presented," he announced, "the babies will be baptized at both the north and south ends of the church."

Hence, the babies were baptized at both ends.

The director of religious education, was the proud mother of five children, four girls and a boy.

At lunch one day at her home with a friend, she was sharing how her child-rearing practices had changed over the years. She reflected on how obsessive she was over her first-born. When that child showed even the slightest sign of a cold or other minor ailment, she said, she would rush her to the doctor.

But that was then and this was now. When her youngest daughter came rushing into the kitchen to inform her mother that she had swallowed a quarter, the mom didn't even look up. "Just remember," she said, "it's coming out of your allowance."

When the deacon's wife went to the store to buy some underwear for her husband, the clerk asked whether she wanted boxers or jockeys.

She replied, "Depends."

Linda was very attached to her pet dog, Fido.
After Fido died, she resolved never to get another pet. However, after a few months, she felt the need for a pet and went to the local pet store. She examined all the cats and dogs, but wasn't attracted to any of them. The store owner, sensing her disappointment, informed her that he had a very special one-of-a-kind pet—a talking centipede.

Linda looked at the centipede, felt an immediate attraction, and bought it.

On Sunday morning she called to the centipede that it was time to go to church, but got no response. She called again, "Time to go to church!" Still no response. She tried yet another time and finally received a reply.

"Be patient!" the centipede pleaded, "I'm putting on my shoes."

When the heating system broke down during one of the coldest weekends of the year, some witty soul put a sign on the church door: "Many are cold, a few are frozen."

As the years wore on, the retired pastor seemed to become more and more cynical. Whenever someone would say, "I'm going to stop by and see you one of these days," he would respond, "Thanks for warning me."

"When I was ready to pay for my groceries today," the parish secretary complained, "the cashier said, 'Strip down, facing me.'"

"I gave her a startled look and made a mental note to complain to my congressman about Homeland Security going too far. However, I did just as she had instructed. When the hysterical laughter at the store subsided, I realized she was referring to my credit card."

The local bishop had such a reputation for desiring the red hat of a cardinal that some of his flock described him as having "scarlet fever."

Little Janie was talking with her middle-aged teacher. "My mother told me," the girl said, "that the older you get the wiser you get."

Little Janie thought for a moment and then declared, "Mrs. Pierce, you must be brilliant."

"I don't suffer from insanity," a parishioner boasted to the pastoral minister. "I enjoy every minute of it."

Marge shared her experience with her aerobics class for seniors. "I bent, twisted, gyrated, jumped up and down, and perspired for over an hour," she complained, "but by the time I got my new tights on, the class was over."

A young priest from Puerto Rico was assigned to a parish in Buffalo, New York. When the town had its first snowfall that year, he rushed outside to experience it.

The other priests, much too familiar with snow, remained in the warmth of the rectory.

After about half an hour, the young priest came indoors. His confreres asked what he thought of the snow.

"Now I know," he responded, "why Joseph and Mary grabbed the stable when they could!"

———·———

Shirley was preparing her will. She made an appointment with her pastor and told him she had two final requests.

"First," she emphasized, "I want to be cremated. And second, I want my ashes scattered in Wal-Mart."

The pastor was rather surprised. "Why Wal-Mart?" he asked

"That way," she explained, "I'm sure that my daughters will visit me at least twice a week."

———·———

Carla stopped at the parish office after a weekday Mass. "My memory is not as sharp as it used to be," she told the secretary. "Also, my memory is not as sharp as it used to be."

———·———

As the priest was giving a rousing sermon on the holiness of married life, one woman turned to the woman in the pew next to her and stated, "I know as much about eschatology as he knows about marriage."

Jake was concerned that his wife Joan might need a hearing aid. Not quite sure how to approach her, he called the family doctor for advice.

The doctor told him there was a simple informal test Jake could perform to give the doctor a better idea of the severity of her hearing loss.

"Here's what you do," said the doctor. "Stand about forty feet away from her, and, in a normal conversational speaking voice, see if she hears you. If not, reduce your distance to thirty feet, then twenty feet, and so on, until you get a response."

"Good idea," said Jake. "I'll try it."

That evening, when Joan was in the kitchen cooking dinner and he was in the den, Jake said to himself, "I'm about forty feet away. Let's see what happens."

"Honey," he asked in a normal voice, "what's for dinner?"

No response.

Jake took a few steps toward the kitchen until he was about thirty feet away. "Honey," he repeated, "what's for dinner?"

Still no response.

Moving out of the den and into the dining room, Jake was now about twenty feet from his wife. "Honey," he asked again, "what's for dinner?" Again, no response.

Now moving to within ten feet of his wife, he raised his voice. "Honey, what's for dinner?"

Still not getting a response, he walked right behind her. "Honey, what's for dinner?"

With great exasperation, Joan turned and glared at him. "Jake," she shouted at the top of her lungs, "for the fifth time, we're having chicken!"

Horace and Ethel came to the parish office to see Sister Dawne, the pastoral minister. They were in their early nineties and had recently celebrated their seventieth wedding anniversary.

Sister Dawne was completely shocked when they reported that they wanted to get a divorce. "Are you sure?" she asked.

"Yes, we're sure," Ethel replied. "We've been contemplating this for a long time."

"But why now?" Sister Dawne asked incredulously.

"We wanted to wait," Horace chimed in, "until all the kids had left home."

The director of the school choir collected original lyrics and prayers of some of her young students.

- "While shepherds washed their socks at night..."
- "Lead us not into Penn Station..."
- "Give us this day our jelly bread..."

Cardinal Leo Joseph Suenens, one of the "stars" at the Second Vatican Council and a great admirer of St. John XXIII, loved to tell stories about the beloved pope.

One of his favorites was the time the pope told the cardinal that he had been having trouble sleeping because of the great responsibility he felt for the Church. But, he told Cardinal Suenens, he had solved his problem. "I said to myself, you're the pope, I command you to go to sleep. It worked infallibly."

Cathy asked her husband, Brian, "What are you doing to-day?"

"Nothing," he replied.

"That's what you said yesterday."

"I know, but I'm not finished yet."

———

A substitute priest apologized for the brevity of his homily before he even gave it. "Before I left home this morning," he announced, "my pet dog, Bella, chewed up my notes, destroying most of what I was going to say."

As he greeted parishioners after Mass, one woman walked up and whispered in his ear. "If Bella ever has puppies," she confided, "please give one to our pastor."

———

Santa visited the children at their school Christmas party, and Little Jonnie, one of the first-graders, sat on his lap.

As usual, Santa asked the boy, "And what would you like for Christmas?"

Little Jonnie looked at Santa in disbelief and said, "Didn't you get my email?"

———

Sheila decided to have some fun with one of her adult formation classes, asking students to punctuate the following: "Woman without her man is nothing."

The men wrote: "Woman, without her man, is nothing."

The women wrote: "Woman! Without her, man is nothing."

The preacher was winding up his temperance sermon with great fervor. "If I had all the beer in the world," he cried, "I'd take it and throw it into the river."

And the congregation cried, "Amen!"

"And if I had all the wine in the world," he continued, "I'd take it and throw it into the river too."

Again, the congregation cried in unison, "Amen!"

"And if I had all the whiskey and demon rum in the world," he shouted, "I'd take it all and throw it into the river."

The congregation was on its feet now, shouting, "Hallelujah! Hallelujah!"

And the preacher sat down, and the song leader stood up. "Our closing song," she invited, almost sheepishly, "is hymn #365, 'Shall We Gather at the River?'"

"I have a question for you," the brother who loved riddles said to the sister who didn't. "A cowboy rode into town on Friday. He left two days later on Friday. How did he do that?"

The nun grappled with the question for a half hour before finally conceding she had no idea.

"The horse's name," the brother proclaimed, "was Friday."

The bishop shared his impression of seminary training before and after Vatican II: "Prior to Vatican II, it was night prayer and lights out," he said. "Since Vatican II, it's been light prayers and nights out."

Sister Jeanine had just celebrated her fiftieth anniversary as a member of the congregation when she came down with the flu.

The infirmarian at the mother house asked her if she'd like anything to drink. After some reflection, Sister Jeanine asked for a glass of warm milk.

The infirmarian, believing the elderly nun needed something a little stronger, decided to add a half-shot of whiskey.

After Sister Jeanine finished the milk, the infirmarian inquired whether she had any other requests. "Yes," she urged. "Tell the sisters not to sell that cow."

The priest had heard a burglar in the rectory the night before, so that night he hid in a corner of the rectory where he could hear but not be seen.

Trying not to make a sound, he soon heard two voices, the voice of a burglar and the voice of his pet parrot.

The parrot kept repeating, "Jesus is coming. Jesus is coming."

The robber, surprised at first, realized it was a parrot doing the talking. Intrigued, he asked the parrot, "What's your name?"

"Sweetie," the parrot replied.

"What kind of a jerk names his parrot Sweetie?" the robber asked.

"The same jerk who calls his pit bull Jesus," the parrot responded.

The burglar ran out the door.

The priest never did buy a pit bull.

Father Jim noticed Mrs. Sarna sitting in the back of the church. She looked so forlorn that he approached her and asked her what was wrong.

"It's my husband, Father," she said. "He suffers from seasonal depression. He's a Chicago Cubs fan, and midway through the summer he always gets very moody. Is there anything you think would help?"

Father Jim paused for only a second, looked her straight into her eyes, and said, "Patience and hope," he said. "And some decent starting pitching."

In accepting his 1952 Emmy Award for his *Life Is Worthy Living* TV program, Bishop Fulton Sheen gave credit where credit was due. "I feel it is time I pay tribute to my four writers," he said, "Matthew, Mark, Luke, and John."

The parish secretary had been complaining for months that her computer was unbearably slow and was constantly freezing up. Finally, it died.

When the deacon heard the news, he asked if she had tried mouse-to-mouse resuscitation.

A Catholic college student coming home for Christmas constantly wore the same tee shirt. It said, "No, I don't know what's wrong with your computer."

Denise and Helen, two ninety-year-old members of St. Ignatius Parish, had been life-long friends and both loved to cook.

Denise was seriously ill with little hope of recovery. In fact, the doctors did not give her long to live.

One day Helen visited her in the hospital to assure Denise of her prayers and to make a strange request. "Denise," she asked, "when you get to heaven, can you find a way to let me know if there's a kitchen where we can cook?"

Shortly after Helen's visit, Denise died.

A week after the funeral, Helen received a special delivery package. Inside she found some of Denise's favorite cookies and a note that said: "Helen, I've got good news and bad news. The kitchen here is state of the art and free and open to everyone. Just taste these cookies! The bad news is that they've got you scheduled to bake your famous lasagna for next Wednesday's dinner."

———

To some people a priest is invisible six days a week and incomprehensible on the seventh.

———

Question:
What is the course of study
at a Catholic clown college called?
Answer:
A sacred silly-bus.

Sister June had droned on for the entire evening at her religious community's monthly meeting. When she left, there was a sigh of relief.

"I think," said Sister Matilda, "Sister June has said it all."

"Yes," said Sister Anastasia, "there is nun-thing left to say."

Rich, a Catholic elementary school teacher from Brooklyn, was experiencing so much stress that he couldn't sleep at night. He decided to see a Park Avenue psychiatrist, reputedly the best and certainly the most expensive in New York City.

He arrived for his appointment on time and entered a well-furnished reception area. He noticed two doors—one marked *men* and the other marked *women*. Rich opened the door for men and entered a luxurious reception area with two more doors—one marked *over age fifty* and the second *under age fifty*. Since he was forty-two, he again chose the second and entered a room with beautiful art and very comfortable chairs.

Not surprisingly, he found two more doors—the first marked *annual salary over $100,000* and the second marked *annual salary under $100,000*. Since he was a Catholic elementary teacher, he opened the second door and found himself outside the building on Park Avenue.

He slept beautifully that night.

Sign spotted in the cafeteria of the local Catholic high school: "Jesus is coming, and he looks mad!"

One of the teachers from the parish school observed a grandfather and his badly-behaved three-year-old grandson in the supermarket. It was obvious to her that the grandfather had his hands full. The child screamed for sweets in the sweets aisle, reached for cookies in the cookie aisle, and demanded fruit, cereal, and pop.

Meanwhile, the grandfather was working his way around, saying in a controlled voice, "Easy, William, we won't be long. Easy, boy."

After another juvenile outburst, she heard him calmly say, "It's okay, William. Just a couple more minutes, and we'll be out of here. Hang in there, boy."

At the checkout, the little terror was tossing items out of the cart. His grandfather calmly picked them up and said again in a controlled voice, "William, William. Relax, buddy. Don't get upset. We'll be home in five minutes. Stay cool, William."

Very impressed, the teacher followed them to the car. "It's none of my business," she said, "but you were amazing in there. I don't know how you did it. That whole time you kept your composure, and no matter how loud and disruptive he got, you just kept telling William that things would be okay. He is very lucky to have you as his grandpa."

"Thanks," said the grandfather, "but I'm William. The little brat's name is Kevin."

————

Sign seen in front of a Catholic church: "If you feel down in the mouth, have a faith lift."

This is a true story, kind of.
St. John XXIII had endured an extremely chaotic and draining day. When, shortly after dinner, he announced he was going to bed early, his secretary informed him that there was still one group waiting to see him—Catholic press photographers from around the world who were in Rome for their annual convention.

Reluctantly, the pope agreed to meet with them. When he walked into the room, they raised their cameras and almost in unison shouted, "Say cheese."

Cameras clicked and flashed as the pope responded, "Mozzarella!"

Thereafter, he was known as "the Pizza Pope." (That part is not true.)

Mr. Jones, an elderly parishioner, had recently purchased a big-screen TV and accessories to watch his favorite sports.

He drove Mrs. Jones crazy. "He always has it turned up full blast," she complained. "He's high-deaf, you know."

"I overheard some parishioners complaining about your homily on Sunday," said the pastor to his new assistant priest. "They said it was really boring."

"I'm sorry, Father," the young priest responded with genuine remorse. "I had emergency calls at the hospital all day Saturday and didn't have time to prepare, so I just borrowed one of your old ones from the parish website."

Overhead at the weekly senior meeting at the parish hall.

- "Do you know how to prevent sagging? Just eat until the wrinkles fill out."
- "It's scary when you start making the same noises as the coffee maker."
- "These days about half the items in my shopping cart are labeled 'for fast relief.'"
- "Don't let aging get you down. It's too hard to get back up."
- "My husband started walking five miles a day when he was ninety years old. He's now ninety-seven and we have no idea where he is."
- "I like long walks, especially when they are taken by people who annoy me."
- "We all get heavier as we get older because there's a lot more information in our heads."
- "Everything hurts, and what doesn't hurt usually doesn't work."
- "You get a lot of exercise acting as a pallbearer for your friends who didn't exercise."
- "I have too much room in the house and not enough in the medicine cabinet."
- "Your knees buckle, and your belt won't."

**A good preacher is a sophisticated rhetorician
with the exuberance of his own verbosity.**

Sixteen-year-old Bobby had just passed his driver's test. He couldn't wait to tell his father and right away began pressuring his father for use of the family car.

"I'll make a deal with you," his father said to him. "When you bring your grades up from a C to a B average, study the Bible, and get your hair cut, we'll talk about the car."

Bobby hesitated but then agreed, "It's a deal."

A month later Bobby was once again pressuring his father for the use of the car.

" I'm proud of you," said his father. "You've brought your grade average up to a B, and I've observed you reading the Bible, but I'm disappointed that you haven't had your hair cut."

"You know, Dad," Bobby reasoned. "I've been thinking about that. In reading the Bible, I've discovered that Samson had long hair, Moses had long hair, John the Baptist had long hair, and Jesus probably did too."

The father thought for a moment. "You've got a point, son," he said. "Did you also notice that they walked everywhere they went?"

A Catholic couple were expecting their first child and the husband, Mark, was becoming increasingly anxious as they approached the due date.

Finally, when the moment arrived, Mark called the hospital and shouted frantically, "My wife is pregnant and her contractions are only two minutes apart."

"Is this her first child?" the receptionist asked.

"No!" Mark shouted. "This is her husband."

Three Catholics died in a car accident and arrived in heaven at the same time.

St. Peter asked them just one question, "When you are in your casket and your friends are mourning your loss, what would you like to hear them say about you?"

The first one replied, "I would like to hear them say that I was not only a great doctor but also an outstanding family man."

The second one, without hesitation, responded, "I would like to hear them say that I was the best teacher they ever had and that I made a lasting, positive impression on every one of them."

The third man took his time mulling over the question. Then his face brightened and he said, "I would love to hear them say, 'Look! He's moving!'"

———

The seminarian was feeling overwhelmed by the philosophical questions being raised in his classes. One day, he had the bright idea of making a t-shirt with the following wording:

To be or not to be? William Shakespeare
The way to do is to be. Lao-tzu
The way to be is to do. Dale Carnegie
Do-be-do-be-do. Frank Sinatra

———

Question:
When is a door in a church not a door?
Answer:
When it's holy ajar.

Beth, the parish secretary, was feeling pretty discouraged, claiming her heavy workload had led to the recent mistakes in the bulletin:

- Ushers will eat latecomers.
- Remember in your prayers the many people who are sick of our church.
- The eighth-graders will be presenting Shakespeare's Hamlet in the church basement on Friday at 7 p.m. The congregation is invited to attend this tragedy.
- On Tuesday evening there will be a potluck supper. Prayer and medication to follow.
- The pastor will be on vacation for the next two weeks. Massages can be given to the parish secretary.
- The choir invites any member of the congregation who enjoys sinning to join the choir.
- The weight management group will meet at 7 p.m. on Wednesday. Please use the large double doors at the side entrance.

At the parish council meeting, one man boasted to another, "I'm a multi-tasker."

His wife, also on the council, overheard the conversation and turned to her friend, saying, "He thinks muti-tasking is doing the same thing over and over again until he finally gets it right."

Brother John's solution to his mid-life crisis was to have an expensive face lift. He was extremely pleased with the results.

A week later, feeling very proud of himself, he asked the clerk at the ice cream parlor, "How old do you think I am?"

After studying him, the clerk guessed, "I'd say late twenties or early thirties."

Brother John vainly announced, "I'm forty-seven years old."

Still feeling his oats, he stopped at the bakery and asked the baker the same question.

The baker, without hesitation, said, "Thirty."

With a wide smile on his face, the brother informed the baker, "I'm forty-seven."

John then boarded the bus and a woman sat down next to him. "I just had a birthday last week," he said, "and if you can correctly tell me how old I am, I'll give you twenty dollars."

She barely looked up from her knitting. "You are forty-seven years old," she said.

Now deflated, John paid her the twenty dollars. "How did you figure that out?" he asked pathetically. "Do I look forty-seven?"

"No," she responded with a smile. "I was behind you at the bakery."

Priestly wisdom:
When in charge, ponder.
When in trouble, delegate.
When in doubt, mumble.

Quasimodo was the legendary bell-ringer of Notre Dame Cathedral. When he died, the archbishop sent word throughout Paris that he was looking for a new bell-ringer.

One applicant had a rather unique way of getting the most from the beautiful bells. He struck them with his face. He was hired on the spot.

A month later the bell-ringer fell from the tower and died. The archbishop rushed out into the street and saw the bell-ringer lying dead in the midst of a large crowd.

One of the people in the crowd asked the archbishop if he knew who this man was.

"I don't know his name," the archbishop replied, "but his face rings a bell."

Just then a man emerged from the crowd, claiming he was the brother of the dead bell-ringer. He asked if he could have the honor of replacing his brother. The archbishop agreed, telling him of the serious responsibility of the position. They walked together to the top of the tower.

The archbishop watched as the man picked up a huge mallet to strike the bells, suffered a massive heart attack, and dropped dead right on the spot.

Monks from the church came running up into the belfry, observed the dead man lying at the feet of the archbishop, and asked, "Who is this man?"

"I don't know his name," sighed the distraught archbishop, "but he's a dead ringer for his brother."

**The parish nurse set up a weekly exercise program.
People worked out religiously.**

A cardinal archbishop who was getting up in years insisted that he was always right.

One day he told one of his priests that he was making him a monsignor.

When the priest didn't respond, the cardinal was somewhat surprised. "Father," he repeated, "I'm making you a monsignor, and you don't seem to have any reaction. Why is that?"

"Cardinal," the priest replied gently, "you made me a monsignor last year."

To which the cardinal said, "And an excellent decision it was, wouldn't you agree?"

"Yes, Your Eminence," said the priest with a smile.

The Three Bs of Preaching
Be prepared.
Be insightful.
Be seated.

Tom had just been elected president of the pastoral council. In his customary boastful manner he declared, "Cream always rises to the top."

Just out of his hearing, his wife whispered to herself, "And so does hot air."

Whenever the Catholic Church makes a big change, it starts off the official announcement with: "As we have always taught."

A number of priests from various religious congregations in the diocese attended the Forty Hours Devotion at Veil of Veronica's Parish. While they were praying the Divine Office, a fuse blew and all the lights went out.

The Benedictines, without missing a beat, continued praying from memory.

The Jesuits began discussing whether or not the blown fuse meant they were dispensed from the obligation to pray the Office every day.

The Franciscans sang a hymn of praise for God's gift of darkness.

The Dominicans recalled their charism to teach that light is a symbol and sign of the transmission of divine knowledge.

The Carmelites fell into silence, meditating on the dark night with slow, steady breathing.

The pastor of Veil of Veronica's, a diocesan priest, simply stood up, went to the basement, and replaced the fuse.

The young associate pastor came running into the dining room, screaming and shouting.

The pastor, in the middle of his lunch, asked the associate to slow down and tell him what was going on.

"I just heard the news report," the associate said. "The pope has just announced that priests can get married."

"Is that so?" asked the pastor.

"There are only three conditions," continued the associate breathlessly. "One, the priest has to have celebrated his fiftieth anniversary of ordination. Second, he has to be officially retired. And third, he needs his mother's permission."

The deacon won two fifty-yard-line tickets to the Super Bowl. He and his wife were really excited about going.

Sitting next to them at the game was a middle-aged man. Surprisingly, the prime seat next to him was empty. After a while, the deacon's curiosity got the best of him and he asked the man next to him if anyone else was coming.

The man looked sad and explained that he and his wife had come to the Super Bowl every year for the last twenty years, but that his wife had died recently.

"Oh," exclaimed the deacon, kicking into pastoral mode. "I'm so sorry for your loss. But couldn't you get one of your family or friends to come with you today?"

"No," replied the man. "They're all at the funeral."

The pastor came running into the parish office. "Marge," he yelled to the secretary, "I just saw someone stealing your car from the parking lot!"

Marge was shocked and asked, "Did you see who it was?"

"No," he replied, "but I got the license number."

Right before Lent, Sister Maureen asked if anyone knew what *denial* is.

Little Jonnie, who didn't usually have the right answer but was never afraid to try, thought he knew this one.

"Denial, S'ter," he proudly and loudly declared, "is a river in Egypt."

Two of the members of the men's senior club at the parish were sitting next to each other after Monday morning Mass.

One asked his buddy, "Do you have any plans for today?"

"Yes," his friend responded. "I'll be filling up space and taking up time."

Without missing a beat, the first guy answered, "And you do it very well."

———·———

Father John was in his study on Sunday morning praying that God send him some insight on how to raise the money to repair the leaking church roof. His prayer was interrupted by the substitute organist, who wanted to know what songs to play at Mass.

Father John was caught off guard. "Use your own judgment," he instructed brusquely.

After the homily, Father John announced, "We need an additional $4,000 to repair the roof. Any of you who can pledge $100 or more, please stand up."

The substitute organist immediately launched into "The Star Spangled Banner."

And that is how the substitute became the regular organist.

———·———

The priest was accustomed to receiving unsigned mail from disgruntled parishioners complaining about all sorts of things. But even he was surprised when he opened a letter with no return address and a single screw tumbled onto the table. "After listening to your homily on Sunday," the note read, "I decided you must have lost this."

A deacon known for his long homilies was in the middle of one of them when a gust of wind blew through an open window and scattered his pages of notes on the floor.

After picking them up, he placed each page in the correct order. "Now," he asked, "where was I?"

From the first pew came a loud voice, "On the last page!"

The bishop arrived at the parish to celebrate Mass. As he entered the sacristy to vest, he was met by the pastor.

As they entered the church to process, the bishop was surprised to see only one little old lady kneeling and praying her rosary.

Indignant, the bishop turned and demanded of the pastor, "Didn't you tell your people I was coming?"

The pastor looked around at the empty church. "No," he said defensively. "I didn't, but apparently someone else did."

Sign spotted at the local Catholic hospital: "Parking is for small Catholic cars only."

After their Thanksgiving feast, every member of the family, one by one, shared something for which they were thankful.

When it came to Little Janie, the youngest at the table, she folded her hands and bowed her head very piously.

"I'm thankful," she exclaimed with genuine emotion, "I'm not the turkey."

Yahweh handed Moses the two tablets containing the ten commandments.

Moses pondered them for several minutes.

Knowing how Moses' mind worked, Yahweh assured him, "Yes, they've already been run by the legal department."

Two cows were chatting in the monastery's grazing field as they watched trucks pass on the highway.

One truck was plastered with a sign that read "Whole Milk."

The next read "Chocolate Milk."

And the third declared "100% Cream."

One cow glanced at the other cow and said, "I feel udderly inadequate."

Little Janie was going on and on about something that had happened at school that day. Finally, her father stopped her long enough to say, "Little Janie, you sound like a broken record."

Little Janie responded, "What's a record, Dad?"

Brother Jim was driving down the street in a panic. He had an important meeting in ten minutes and couldn't find a parking place. Looking up to heaven, he prayed, "Lord, take pity on me. If you find me a parking place I will give up all alcohol."

Miraculously, a parking place appeared at that very moment.

Brother Jim looked up again. "Never mind, Lord," the brother said with a sigh of relief, "I found one myself."

Overheard from one of the seventh-grade boys in the Catholic school yard: "I can pitch with both my left hand and right hand. I'm amphibious."

Distressed, one of the girls said to him, "But we haven't made our Confirmation yet."

------·------

Little Jonnie went out with his parents for dinner. He was surprisingly well-behaved throughout the meal, but he asked his dad why they couldn't bring their dog, Rex.

The father said that it wasn't appropriate to bring dogs to a restaurant.

At the end of the meal, the father asked the waitress for a doggie bag.

Now Little Jonnie was totally confused. "How come, Dad," he asked, "Rex never gets to come to the restaurant and then he never gets to eat what's in the doggie bag?

------·------

Bernice, a fawning grandmother, always sat at the same table at the monthly parish card party. She was determined to prove the superiority of her two grandchildren.

Laura, joining the table for the first time, noticed that Bernice had her wallet open and was showing pictures of her two grandchildren. Naturally, she asked about them. The other women at the table shook their heads.

Bernice proudly showed Laura the picture of a three-year-old boy and four-year-old girl. "This is Martin and Michelle," she boasted. "He's a doctor and she's a lawyer."

The man insisted that his son, a renowned surgeon, perform his operation.

Just as he was being administered the anesthesia, he asked to speak to his son.

"Yes, Dad, what is it?"

"Don't be nervous, Son," he assured him." Do your best and just remember: If it doesn't go well and anything happens to me, your mother is going to come live with you and your wife."

The man came through the operation with flying colors.

Jesuit psychiatrist Father James Gill had many interesting experiences during his medical residency.

One day he was with a Catholic patient when the man went into cardiac arrest. He immediately called a Code-4 and adjusted the bed so that the patient was flat on his back. Then he knelt on the bed and started CPR. While he was doing chest compressions with both hands, it suddenly occurred to him that the man may not have been anointed. So he continued CPR with his left hand while freeing his right hand to make the sign of the cross over the patient.

Just then members of the cardiac response team, including a fellow resident, rushed into the room. Seeing Father Jim doing double-duty—blessing and resuscitating—the colleague exclaimed, "Geez, Jim, you refuse to lose one, don't you?"

The pastor made an announcement after his homily. "I have good news and bad news," he said. "The good news is we have enough money to pay for our new building program. The bad news is the money's still in your pockets."

———

Maggie was chatting with Linda at a meeting of the parish staff. After showing Linda some pictures of her new grandchild, Maggie wistfully declared, "If I had known how much fun grand-children were going to be, I would have had them first."

———

Catherine, having reached the grand age of eighty, had just gotten married for the fourth time.

A reporter from the local paper was assigned to ask her questions about her life, her recent marriage, and her new husband's occupation.

"He's a funeral director," she answered.

Interesting, the reporter thought. "Can you tell me a little about your first three husbands and what they did for a living?"

Catherine paused for a few moments, reflecting on all those happy years, then she smiled and she answered proudly, "I married a banker when I was in my twenties, a circus ringmaster in my forties, and a preacher in my sixties. And now, as you know, I have married a funeral director as I begin my eighties."

The interviewer looked at her, quite astonished. "Why," he asked, "would you marry men with such diverse careers?"

Catherine paused for a quick beat for effect and then said: "It's obvious, isn't it? One for the money. Two for the show. Three to get ready. And four to go."

During his homily, Father Joel asked, "How many of you have forgiven your enemies?"

Everyone except Mr. Barnes raised their hands.

"Mr. Barnes," the priest asked, "are you not willing to forgive your enemies?"

"I don't have any," he replied gruffly from his pew.

"Mr. Barnes, that is very unusual," the priest mused. "How old are you?"

"Ninety-eight," he replied.

"Would you mind coming up here," Father Joel said, inviting the man up to the pulpit, "to tell us how a person can live ninety-eight years and not have any enemies?"

Mr. Barnes tottered up the aisle, stopped at the pulpit, and announced simply, "I outlived them all." Then he returned to his seat to thunderous applause.

Patrick was visiting family in New York City from Ireland. He patiently waited while the cop on Fifth Avenue near the cathedral directed traffic, stopping cars from time to time and shouting, "Okay, pedestrians," and waving them across.

All the people waiting crossed the street before the officer signaled the cars to proceed. He'd done this several times, but Patrick was still standing on the curb.

After the cop had shouted, "Okay, pedestrians!" for the tenth time, Patrick went over to him and complained, "Sure and isn't it about about time," he asked the police officer, "that you let the Catholics across?"

Two Catholic guys from different parishes were pushing their carts around Wal-Mart when they collided.

"Sorry about that," said the one. "I'm looking for my wife and I guess I wasn't paying attention to where I was going."

"That's okay," said the other. "What a coincidence. I'm looking for my wife, too. I can't find her, and I'm getting a little desperate."

"Well, maybe I can help you find her," offered the first. "What does she look like?"

"Well," said the second. "She's twenty-seven years old and quite tall. She has beautiful red hair, blue eyes, long legs, and is wearing short shorts. What does your wife look like?"

"Doesn't matter," said the first. "Let's look for your poor wife first."

Patricia was mailing the family Bible to her cousin, who wanted to have it for his swearing in as a judge.

"Is there anything breakable in here?" asked the postal clerk.

"Just the Ten Commandments," Patricia answered.

Two brothers were discussing computers and their own failing memory.

"I finally found the perfect password: *incorrect*," one said. "Every time I type in what I think is my password, the computer informs me, 'Your password is incorrect.'"

Dom and Sal, the maintenance men at a Catholic school, were standing at the base of the school flagpole, looking up. One of the school mothers walked by and asked what they were doing.

"For some reason the principal wants us to find out the height of this flagpole," said Dom, "but we don't have a ladder that high."

The woman took a wrench and tape measure from her purse. She had the two guys loosen some bolts and lay the pole down on the ground. Then she used the tape measure and announced, "Twenty-one feet, six inches," and walked away.

Sal shook his head and laughed. "Ain't that just like a woman?" he said. "We ask for the height and she gives us the length."

———

Question:
What did Moses use to illuminate his ark at night?
Answer:
Moses wasn't on the ark.

Question:
OK, then what did Noah use to illuminate the ark?
Answer:
Flood lights. What else would he have used?

———

The deacon found a message taped to the pulpit that read, "Be memorable, not eternal."

Barbara and Raymond were sitting on a swing on the front porch enjoying a glass of ice tea.

Barbara looked over at Raymond. Seeing his eyes were closed, she asked, "Are you asleep?"

With the eyes still closed, Raymond responded, "No, I'm just contemplating."

"Contemplating what?" asked Barbara.

"The big question," responded Raymond. "Why am I here?"

Barbara looked wistfully into the sky. "I often ask myself that same question," she sighed. "Why are you here?"

———

When Gil opened the morning newspaper, he was dumbfounded to find his death notice in the obituary column. He quickly phoned his best friend, Chris.

"Did you see the paper?' asked Gil. "It says I died!"

"Yes, I saw it, replied Chris. "Where are you calling from?"

———

As he walked into the bar, Ben said to the bartender, "Pour me a stiff one, Charlie. I just had another fight with the little woman."

"Oh yeah?" said Charlie. "And how did this one end?"

"When it was over," Ben replied, "she came to me on her hands and knees."

"Really?" said Charlie, "Now that's a switch! What did she say?"

"She said, 'Come out from under that bed, you little chicken.'"

The pastor had been complaining to his staff that his cold and sinus congestion made it impossible for him to sleep. One night, however, he discovered that if he sat up in bed, he felt better and was eventually able to fall asleep.

The next morning, he announced at the staff meeting that he was designing a bed that enabled the sleeper to sit perfectly upright. He went on and on about his idea and what he might call it.

After listening for fifteen minutes, the parish secretary burst his bubble, saying, "Father, why don't you just call it a chair?"

What do the angels say when God sneezes?
"Bless yourself."
"Godzundheit."
"What was *that*?"

Rosie and Terry were babysitting their grandchild, Little Jonnie, a six-year-old.

The boy approached his grandfather and asked, "Can you make that sound like a frog?"

Terry was completely confused. "What are you talking about?" he asked.

"Grandma said that when you croak," he replied, "we are all going to go to Disneyland."

Lloyd and Lynn, who were expecting their first child, attended Lamaze classes held at their parish. The parish nurse conducting the course instructed everyone, "Ladies, remember that exercise is good for you. Walking is especially beneficial. It strengthens the pelvic muscles and will make delivery that much easier. Just pace yourself, make plenty of stops, and try to stay on a soft surface like grass."

"Gentlemen," she continued, "remember you two are in this together. It wouldn't hurt you to go walking with your wife. In fact, that shared experience would be good for you both."

At this point, Lloyd raised his hand. "I was just wondering," he asked. "Would it be helpful if my wife carries a golf bag while we walk?"

To which the parish nurse responded, "It won't hurt the baby, but you might get a headache."

After God created Adam, he realized that Adam was a lonely man. So God said, "Adam, it is not right that you should be alone. I will create a woman, and you shall have someone who will love you and care for you, someone to share your life."

Adam's face lit up. "God, that's wonderful," he said. "A woman would make me very happy, and I would no longer be lonely. Thank you, God."

As Adam began to think about his new life, a question popped into his head. "God," he asked, "what will this cost me?"

God's answer was immediate and concise. "An arm and a leg."

Adam was sad as he thought of the consequences. Suddenly his face lit up again. "What can I get for a rib?"

The pastor was visiting the new family in the parish. During the entire visit, the six-year-old daughter, Little Janie, kept staring at his Roman collar.

The priest finally pointed to his collar and asked Little Janie if she knew what it was.

"Yes," replied Little Janie with confidence. "It keeps fleas and ticks away for up to thirty days."

———·—

Brother Loughlan awoke suddenly one morning and glanced at the clock on his bedside table. The time was 7:07. He got dressed and headed for the bus to go to work. When he boarded the bus, he noticed that it was number 777. Due to construction, the bus was much slower than usual, and he arrived at the office seven minutes late. Brother Loughlan, a superstitious man, concluded that God was giving him a message.

At lunch time he went to the off-track betting office to place a bet on the horses. Lo and behold! The seventh race listed Lucky Sevens as the #7 horse with odds of 7-1. He ran to the window, took a hundred dollar bill out of his billfold, and bet the entire amount on Lucky Sevens with odds of 7 to 1. Brother Loughlan was ecstatic, truly believing that God was guiding him.

When he returned home from work, he immediately went online to get the race results. Lucky Sevens, he discovered, had come in seventh.

Family and friends gathered at the Catholic senior living center to celebrate Betty's one-hundredth birthday. Naturally, someone asked her the secret of making it to the century mark.

"It's simple," Betty said. "Just get to ninety-nine, and then be very careful for the next 365 days."

One day around Christmas, Little Jonnie returned home from Mass and told his mother he wanted to join the children's choir. In fact, he told her, he already knew the words of one of the hymns they had sung that morning.

"That's wonderful, Little Jonnie," his mother replied. "What song did you learn?"

Still beaming, Little Jonnie replied, "Lasagna in the highest."

Andrew, a deacon candidate, was feeling extremely anxious as he accompanied Deacon Joe on a hospital call.

When Deacon Joe asked Andrew to say a prayer over the ailing parishioner, he got flustered. "Eternal rest," he began. Realizing his mistake, he then continued, "Bless us, O Lord...."

At this point, the parishioner opened her eyes and kindly suggested Andrew might try a different ministry. Perhaps something in the food industry, or writing joke books.

ACKNOWLEDGMENTS

I am deeply indebted to Greg Pierce and Patricia Lynch of ACTA Publications for their encouragement, support, and editorial assistance.

Special thanks to my friend, Helen Osman, Secretary of Communications of the United States Conference of Catholic Bishops for writing the Foreword.

I am especially grateful to Dawne Fleri, who used her special gift of writing to edit the manuscript and offer valuable suggestions, as well as to Sister Carroll Juliano, SHCJ.

Some of my friends and relatives and confreres contributed their favorite jokes and stories to this volume: Linda Amadeo; Archbishop Gregory Aymond; Father William Burkert; Father Anselm Deehr, ST; Dawne Fleri; Myrna Gallagher; Sister Ellen Kieran, MSBT; Brother Richard McCann, ST; Anne Mescal; Brother Hiliary Mettes, ST; Terri Nelson; John Osman; Brother Howard Piller, ST; Father Conrad Schmitt, ST; Father Thadeus Searles, ST; and Raymond Sofield. I also stole a few jokes from Deacon Tom Sheridan's four *Books of Catholic Jokes*, but I figure he stole them from someone else anyway.

ABOUT THE AUTHOR

Brother Loughlan Sofield, ST, has been a member of the Missionary Servants of the Most Holy Trinity for over fifty-five years and is currently the director of the order's retirement community.

He spends time on the road working with dioceses, parishes, and other Catholic institutions. To date he has worked in almost three hundred dioceses on six continents.

Brother Loughlan was Senior Editor of *Human Development* magazine for over thirty years and served as a member of the Advisory Board of the National Conference of Catholic Bishops' Committee on Laity, Family, Women, and Youth.

He has been the recipient of a number of awards, including *Lumen Gentium*, conferred by the Conference for Pastoral Planning and Council Development on an individual "who has implemented the direction and goals of the Second Vatican Council in an extraordinary manner," and the National Association of Lay Ministry's *Gaudium et Spes* award, presented to someone who has "evidenced to the vision of Church articulated in the documents of the Second Vatican Council and who in a special way has advocated and fostered the enhanced role of laity."

He is also the recipient of the "Pie in the Face" Award for worst joke book of the century, given for the first and last time by the Association for the Preservation of Seriousness, Solemnity, and Self-Importance in the Roman Catholic Church.

ALSO AVAILABLE

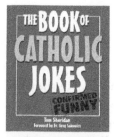

The Book of Catholic Jokes
Deacon Tom Sheridan
Foreword by Fr. Greg Sakowicz
96 pages, paperback

The Second Book of Catholic Jokes
Deacon Tom Sheridan
Foreword by Fr. Paul Boudreau
96 pages, paperback

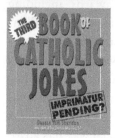

The Third Book of Catholic Jokes
Deacon Tom Sheridan
Foreword by Fr. James Martin, SJ
96 pages, paperback

The Last Book of Catholic Jokes
Deacon Tom Sheridan
Foreword by Sr. Mary Kathleen Glavich, SND
88 pages, paperback

Available from Bookstores or from ACTA Publications
www.actapublications.com 800-397-2282